TO SET RIGHT

Cover image
Alastair Strachan
Daffodils in Sunlight
Collage
25 x 20 cm

Line art
Mirko Velimirović

Cover | Design | Concept
Faride Mereb

Lynne Shapiro

TO SET RIGHT

ISBN: 9781625493866

WordTech Editions
P.O. Box 541106
Cincinnati, OH 45254-1106

www.wordtechweb.com

Poetry Editor: Kevin Walzer
Business Editor: Lori Jareo

"rectyfye and amende Thynges that are amys" — JOHN SKELTON

CONTENTS

8

With the forest high above
I listen hard   to the earth,
          feel vulnerable to any footsteps
that come this way.
Like lotus seeds   in the muck
          my ears are waiting.
Centuries replay as night sweats,
equilibriums   spin   like vinyl records.
What keeps us safe?
What keeps us from stinging bullies
and their need to win at any cost?

Words elude, rotate
like flies   over the carcass of dying winter.
During the war   Kurt Schwitters
cut   his own collages
in order to
          collage again.
Perhaps I should recycle
my own verses,   capitalize on the tension
          of bricolage
to feel productive again.

Today's light tells us   the bees are stirring.
In the interim   we came undone,
and spring's now
          our best hope   for normalcy.
We are tipsy
from what emerges   from the rubble.
Our collective equilibrium's
gone haywire.   Ground is no longer
ground.   We stand on it   but it hovers
before our eyes,
          on a plane of confrontation.

In the pungent leaf-littered understory
          we catch glimpses of   crocheted bits of memory

9

EAR TO THE GROUND

hexed mesh   and fallen apples that   tumble
unseen, hard curves turned spotted
brown, then   melt   into the topsoil
of earth's unspoken promise:

      to grow again
in concert with the bees.
If only their propolis,
could cleanse   and weatherproof   our lives,
      for we've been dirtied   and are hanging
onto civility   only to wonder
if grace matters anymore.

Vertigo is filmic. Labyrinthitis, poetic.
Vestibular neuritis — sweep it under the rug,
compartmentalize it in the vestibule
      of inner sanctums.   What has been buried
now pushes up   through softening soil.
As a child, I played with a plastic uterus
I believed was a beatific inner ear —
canal   and portal.
I felt love   as my father looked inside
with his warm   otoscope light   and at bedtime
when my mother tugged my ears   toward
the light   to see what vegetables needed tending
in my inner garden.

We were once bees: hive clans
      that lost our way   forgot our stories
after centuries   of splitting
like swarming atoms.
Now I'm spinning. Vertigo lurks within
like varroa mites in hives.
I'm too shaky   too worn   too small
to set the world right.
Please
      send in   the bees.

Rag doll
   in a City Line Five & Ten,
     shelved so high,
her features
I could not grasp until in hand:
   painted blue eyes
     yellow braids
       a calico babushka on her head
   and then—
     her skirt raised,
on her back thigh   black stamped letters:

P - O - L - A - N - D.

A landsman,
  like Grandpa!
"Grandma, I need to take her home!"
Too young
   to be told why not —
I sensed   my grandmother's odd reserve
as we stood in line   to pay.

Sometime later, this happened:
Bobby and Magda
grabbed me   raised
  and held my dress   over my head.
Street air   on my underpants
offended me   until I wriggled loose.
But these words spilled out
having risen
from god knows where:
   Jew, you cannot play,
  cannot come into our yards.

Then it was over.
I went home,
spoke not a word
    to them — nor to my Grandma,
who wondered why I'd come inside
 on such a beautiful morning
but who sensed   in me
something
    she did not   recognize.

July was marked
         by writhing groups,
   of *Croatalus horridus*   timber rattlers
   congregated   on the dusty road   to the cabin
   in primordial tangles
beneath the blueberry bush   by the dock.

But it was the one quicksilver snake   that traversed
         in sinuous silence
      the shaded bed   of dry brown leaves   that overlooked
         the lake,   a dammed portion of the Rockaway River   really.

         I no longer recall the particulars   not its color
            though the leaves lie there still (surely different ones now),
         nor how it held its rattle   but it floated
      seemed to float   above ground
   and that led me to move closer   to watch
            despite fear.

   Despite my presence
the snake never changed course   lured along
      by an unknowable intention.

      Children's voices swam in the distance,
         time stopped   stretched
         enough for me to   be alone   with the snake,
            then with one neighbor   then another.
               Each to stand beside me   and gaze.   Time enough
         to phone a snake handler
         and find no one home.   Time enough for the children
   to exit the water   and take a look. And in all that time   the rattler never
changed course.   How I took leave
   of such uncommon beauty
I do not recall.   I suppose it passed   some boundary.
      The old outhouse?   The edge of our property
         where cover gives way   to clearing?

SUMMER OF SNAKES

Too,   it was getting on   late afternoon,
   time for birthday cake and lemonade
  time for the neighbors
 to return to their cabins,
 time for me to recognize ... happiness.

But soon after   the neighbor boy
   rushed in   screen door banging shut   to announce
      his father   had taken an axe   whacked off
        the head   of a snake   the snake his sister almost
      stepped on.
        Almost.
        Did he think
        killing it
           would make him ever safer?

           Within the hour   the family was packed
              returned to the city
             the weekend over
            a severed snake near the woodpile.

      I will never let go   the pure energy,
        how it coursed before me,
       extinguished
      by a man who'd   moments earlier   stood
    in friendship   and awe
        on my land
           but with an axe   on his.

1.

In Sefrou, Morocco, the medina birdman became a friend.
His doves and pigeons were happy, hand raised, generations
of mothers, daughters, fathers, and sons.

One day, walking by, I sensed a new intensity:
two wild English tits batted relentlessly against the bars,
urgently seeking escape.

Why were they in cages?
Les gens aiment leur chanson.
How much are they?
Huit euros.

I'd be back within an hour to buy both.
When I returned, one bird was gone, sold;
the other, mine.
Joyous friends climbed with me to our rooftop to release
the bird, but I was shaken, couldn't forget the other,
even as I replayed the freed bird's unrestricted flight
and glorious song as it perched in a nearby tree.

2.

Landgoed Zonheuvel, Dorn, The Netherlands:
It was in the culminating minutes
of a pioneering global conference, basking
in joy, pondering all the lovely bee people, gratified
for their diversity, their sharing of wisdom (and love),
that we learned of the 12 Palestinian beekeepers who
should have been there with us,
who'd intended to join the conference,
join the Israelis.

The dream I didn't know I had, vaporized in midair
like virga rain, gone before it touches the earth.
Joy ... diminished. The 12 Palestinians weigh heavily,

REVERENCE FOR BEES AND BEING(S)

as I replay the beatific conference in my mind over the past months,
as I read about Gaza and Nablus in the newspaper.

3.

Translated from the Dutch:

You have not provided proof of sufficient means of subsistence.

Your intention to leave the territory before the expiry of the visa could not be ascertained.

Your prompt return following the conclusion of your intended stay cannot be ensured.

In determining where there is a risk of illegal migration, immigration authorities examine the local and general situation in your country of origin.

ENTRY DENIED.

4.

Lila Abass

Fatinah Khatib

Yasmina Khatib

Rodaina Milhim

Manal Noaman

Abed Salam Shaban

Haitham Shaban

Khitam Kamil Shaban

Loai Shaban

Sajida Shaban

Souhad Shaban

Alaa Yousef

NAMES. MORE THAN NAMES.

The passport picture of Souhad from Nablus appears as I open an email.
Sweet face looks out at me. Hajib-framed, like a precious cameo. She does not
know how much I wish she could have been in Dorn, singing, eating,
learning with us. Yossi Aud of Bees for Peace in a letter to Heidi Herrmann:
Five of them invested considerable money in submitting applications, obtaining documents,
translating the application, travel insurance and more.
The others did not come to the embassy for an interview ... when they saw the answers of the
others were not forthcoming and even refused.

Some of the participants (Arab residents of Israel), who are not obligated to a visa,
cancelled ... in solidarity with the others.

5.

Thinking about the Palestinian beekeepers and Bees for Peace

as I watched an Italian–Spanish film, *Les Unwanted De Europa,*

as I read January Gill O'Neil's poem "Hoodie." The last line:

Who could mistake you for anything but good?

as I pondered Timothy Snyder's relevant words: "We can't respond to fear. We must realize it is freedom that matters all the more."

as I imagined Martin Luther King Jr.'s visit to the Berlin Wall, 1964, when he spoke about the "ministry of reconciliation" and his hope that people could "transcend the narrow confines of nationalism."

as Langston Hughes' poem "Harlem" popped into my head repeatedly:

What happens to a dream deferred?

as I read Palestinian poet Mamoud Darwish's "If I were to start all over again I'd choose what I had chosen: The roses on the fence."

as I read Katie Kitamura's review of *The White Book* by South Korean author Han Kang: "Kang explores occupation in multiple forms and contexts, from the Japanese occupation to political demonstrations, always tracing the 'radioactive spread' of trauma. But she also makes a case for empathy. *I saw differently when I looked with your eyes....*"

as I hear Robert Frost reading, "Something there is that doesn't love a wall."

as I think about Paul Éluard's Poems for Peace.

6.

We wanted to smile, shake hands, peer into your eyes, welcome you, tell you we had been waiting for you. We are still waiting for you.

إن شاء الله   incha'Allah / inshallah

Another time will come, another chance to meet, another place.

We will speak out on your behalf, now that we know who you are.

7.

Re- [pair]: to pair again

Kintsugi, also known as Kintsukuroi, is the Japanese art

of repairing broken pottery with lacquer dusted or mixed

with powdered gold. ... It treats breakage and repair as part
of the history of an object, rather than something to disguise.

Not whitewash. (God knows the impossibility of this.)
Paired for all eternity, like topsy-turvy dolls joined at the hip,
twined in conflict, land rifts and land grabs,
cracks in civility, historical mistakes, immoral walls —
the fault lines of blame and mistrust.

Leave scars intact, proof of past, of breakage, of sorrow
and inevitable hope: gold and lacquer, honey and propolis,
heal, mend.

Kintsugi reflects a world too complex for simple answers
and yet — what is simpler
than the scent of almonds in bloom,
the sound of bees in our gardens
the spontaneous celebrations of family,
lunches with friends, sweet traditions
that remind us of love and loss?

8.
We dream of a nation of bees
anticipating the spring
in a golden global hive.

Caterpillars, tiny astronauts,
harness themselves to fate,

wriggle free from earthly suits
to enter an orbital sleep

wherein days and months pass
and bodies melt away.

When cocoons darken,
capsule doors will soon pop open.

Out will come a crumpled, spindly-legged
creature, newly awakened to flight;

left behind — within the still-tethered,
empty pupa — a tiny drop of Milky Way.

19

Inspired by Josef Albers and Brian Eno

20

HOMAGE TO THE SQUARE, RYNEK GLOWNY, KRAKÓW

All the ladies in the square in flouncy orange
dresses, *tanz*-dance the orange, dressed in orange,
spin near Cloth Hall's sunlit brick walls and whisper,
with Helena Rubinstein Nude Glowy lips,

like partners, move to the music
as each shade slips in and out
of classification on the color wheel
of the ceaselessly changing square.

beside the cool-down reddening walls
of a summer night's measured descent.
The show was quite relentless:
color, adjacent to color, arm in arm

to one another and their blue-suited men.
The colors — blue suits, luscious lips, and tangerine dresses —
change as often as dancers swap partners.
The orange dresses become ever hotter hues

22

Or a map,
    breadcrumbs,
        a way out,
a way back.

In Santa Lucia, near Vejer, the scarlet
hibiscus unfurls with first light
    folds   like an umbrella
    with setting sun.   Aperture,
unseen,
remembered,
like the garden, the first garden,
    the garden within.

Lately, the lyric is absent.
Poetry feels too pretty,
    like ballet,
seems beside the point,
    too too clever,
overwrought.
Now I too am vanished
    between cupboard and sink, lost
in quarantine to sanitizing
    and serving.
To keep peace, I try on   the rhythm of others
but that doesn't stop
    the unintended trampling of toes.

Then, I remember to remember.

Lynne, look to the sky.
There are birds, lots of them.
Lots of them.
Migrating

I'm in the hibiscus garden.
I hear Pol's voice and look up.

23

MAY THIS POEM BE A PORTAL

It's the autumnal flight of storks,
the world   without end.
Throngs pass, and
pass, proudly.
Stretches   of joyous configurations
continue without pause.
When the carpet of birds   begins to thin,
the storks swirl round and round,
waiting for the last bird
who searches for possible stragglers
     before they move on
into the paleness beyond sight.

The pageantry gone, I'm exhausted
and ache   from the affliction
of having seen   too much beauty,
Stendhal syndrome,
     like swallowing too much air.

I lay on the grass,   arms
outstretched,
try on   the fanfare
of the southbound muster,
join *Ciconia ciconia*'s
endless ribbon,
and relive the raucous freedom
of convergence
from all points north
in congregation
for the great migration
over the Strait of Gibraltar —
just a few miles away,

each bird having birthed,
or having been born,
     into this ecstatic crossing.

Their journey   a reverse of mine.
I ferried from Tangier to Tarifa
to the hibiscus garden's house
on a floating portal   across the Strait,
amidst hundreds   of immigrant families
whose tongues spoke   every possibility,
who converged from various lands like the storks.
My ears, whirling pistils of receptivity,
heard angelic voices as I merged,
and recalled how I merged,
with that abundant phalanx
of boundless life —

benediction.

26

She didn't say why not
but I sensed   an absence of   joy,
a chill in the particulars that revolved
around my grandma   the doll
     with braids and babushka
that I took home anyway.

Years passed.

At dinner,   talk of Poland.
I beg my husband to join me.   *I'll go …*

he pauses

… but don't expect me   to feel your joy.

And at that my   husband and grandma
who never met
     fall into holy alignment.

His words and her demeanor in the store
like systemic overlays
     in my father's medical books,
like the classic TV game show *Concentration* —
     a match is made   and the board opens up
to reveal   a puzzle part —
like a surveillance photo   that aligns
with a pilot's view of earth
     and triggers   a missile drop.

Explosions all.

How long can it take for impact to propel forward?

Each decade   we put Łódź behind us.
My mom married, divorced, remarried.

We moved from Queens to California,
took the grandparents with us.
I grew, graduated, moved East,
married, raised a child.

After our talk of Poland   a hazy memory
tugged at me, worked me over for days
until a brief moment became vivid and clear.
Until the doll came back
I could never explain   how I felt no hate,
that I loved pierogies, mushrooms, and borscht
and dreamt of Łódź, HollyŁódź —
my grandfather's city —
Piotrkowska Street
with cafes and conversations,
apartment with inner-facing courtyards
and lace curtains,
and visits with   aunts and uncles
     I never met
all dead   some buried
in soil that waits for me.

Moss grows on *matzeva*
　　like pincushions in tailor shops.
Twilight. Fireflies wink in the ghetto field
as I set out
to meet unlikely friends
　　second-growth ghosts
　　　　within　　and without　　the cemetery gates.

　　　　　　　I take leave of the seder table,
　　　　　　　where the Haggadah is read like stale crumbs,
　　　　　　　to walk among my real family.

In the dark　　distances shrink.
Unclear words　　flung like books
land before me　　on cobblestones
amid rustling skirts and heels.

Who will meet me at the threshold?
How will I make myself known?

Inscriptions　　in Hebrew
that I cannot read.
Son of Cwi and Nacha
daughter of Jakob and Malka
partitioned by gender
engraved birth and death years
some embroidered with palms　　and　　stars
burning candles　　or rows of books.

　　　　　　　I raise my glass,　　dip　　my finger in wine
　　　　　　　remove, drip by bloody drip,
　　　　　　　　　the ancient plagues
　　　　　　　onto my dinner plate.

Do pastoral aprons bind us still
　　to unfinished chores and　　inward-facing courtyards?
　　　Each sip of wine　　*Baruch atah*　　thimblefuls of memory.

How to reconnect to this land of milking and murder?
Measure the lichen — indicator of good health, blessings.
Measure the wind in the field
     like a needle coursing through silk.

I run my fingers   over the tablecloth   hem.

Why is this night different from all other nights?

A final scene with no verbs.   I find myself
in the cold   sowing seeds
placing stones
     like buttons   whispering
     in that haunted language   so I can reconcile
     parents with their children   and children with parents
     be my grandfather's emissary.

My brother-in-law reads the Hebrew.
Someone asks in English,
Who will open   the door   for Elijah?

No one notices
that I've already
     let in the ghosts.

Lean in to see out as the train slows,
glass becomes framed mirror.

Greenery becomes you, flannel caresses your one-time youth.
How liquid we are, here and gone, broken open by dappled green,

engulfed by revered fusion of beauty and its opposite,
periphery and its opposite, interiority and its opposite.

The window of plenty induces emerald ecstacy.
Pinholes of the past collide in the lush tracery. Liquid jade

hardens into something you can hold onto when the train rolls
to a stop. If I lived here, would I be like ivy?

Warm light enfolds like a blanket in a greenhouse.
From deep within the public address, missives blare, to remind us

there are schedules to keep, the track goes both ways,
and there's another you up ahead.

TRACK SIGNALS

32

Who slept in this attic before me,
how many in line for their lives?
I'll retrace their steps tomorrow,
peer down into their mass grave,
travel the short distance to Ponar Forest.

But now it's twilight in my room.
The clatter of silverware and platters.
Giggles. Footsteps on cobblestones.
Swifts chatter and call to one another,
loop clouds, darkening coverlets for sleepyheads.

The insects that began their songs at dusk
are suddenly absent —
I remember the grasshopper beside me
after a nap, back home, three limbs gone,
shed from one side of its tiny body
in instinctual escape. Still alive.

33

At Ponar, beneath the towering pines, how many
mothers stepped from skirts and slips, shoes
and stockings to silently relinquish their babies
to still-warm piles of clothing
so to face the pit's black edge
with empty arms and a heart still beating
with a modicum of hope.

34

Only horizon   for bearings
slight breeze
pale pink   water   mimics sky
        no ripples
    calm

            and then
    the ocean
            as I'd seen it   as a child

arms outstretched

my grandma and I   drifted
            near the offing   edge
                where world   drops
                        off and away
                and I felt no fear

                no fear then.

36

Budding roses burst through the window screen,

anchored themselves

in the darkened room above his head.

My grandfather, propped in his chair,

entered a pantomime.

Without waking, he unfurled

thread from a spool, cut it with his teeth,

threaded a needle, pulled taut

his dance partner.

Then he pinched tobacco

from a pouch, packed a pipe, lit a match,

drew on the mouthpiece of his turbaned meerschaum

without waking.

He inhaled; the room rose and fell,

an exchange of air,

the scent of loved ones.

Mingled with exhalations, remembrances:

the pressure cooker

the meat grinder

Sunday sweetbreads, *forshpeiz*

Grandma's polka-dot dress

her pocketbook with Chiclets and

lipstick-smeared white knit gloves

dominoes

the three sailor boys gone to war

his sisters lost to smoke

the only girl, my mother,

the middle room where Bernie was born

opera on the radio

the Yiddish *Forverts*

On the mantel, a photo:

He's dancing with my grandmother,

they face one another

hands held high

poised to cross the dance floor

for the next fifty years.

SMOKE

MY GRANDFATHER'S

He put down hammer and nails,
finished laying the banquet floor
in time for his wedding.
On it, he stands, a boy, a man,
in prayer, with eyes closed
until the breaking of glass.

His father takes his white wedding shirt
within his fingers, works the buttons
one by one, tenderly,
wraps the wide black cloth round
and round and round
his son's birth line.

The groom's heart enters
the black coat, his soul the hat;
he is readied to
walk within the fathers'
guiding light to the huppah.

The bride traces
the belt's centrifugal course,
walks round and round the groom
to stand beside him
on the ground he laid,
becoming herself a belt,
the way story surrounds story
in the Talmud,
the way everything blooms
from the inside out.

SISTER'S GREAT–GREAT–GRANDSON'S

She takes me by the hand,
seats me with her five sisters
opposite rows of fedoras and fur
in a garden of tailored gowns.

Around the huppah, the bride journeys
seven times, escorted by
maternal illumination
to stand at the threshold
where the roof retracts,
opens to the heaven above heaven.

The sisters draw me close,
whisper in honeysuckle:
This be the holiest of times.
Generations of ancestors have descended
right now, ten generations in this room.
And they know you are here with us too.

I hear rustling fabric
and shuffling shoes.
Can unseen thread really restore
what has been severed?

WEDDING, BOROUGH PARK, BROOKLYN

I believe I am on the trail
of the family.

Cannot find current
listings but Interior

Ministry whom I
can visit
on Sunday

may hold answer

with Population
Registry information

they can
provide to a

citizen (me).

If I am correct then
whole matter should
take five hours
or less even
with phone call

to gauge
receptivity and
ensure it is
correct family.

If I am wrong

It will take less

but you will
have struck
out.

He put down hammer and nails
finished laying the banquet hall floor
In time for his own wedding.
On it, he stands a boy, a son,
in prayer, with eyes closed
until the breaking
of the glass under his foot.

His father
takes his white wedding shirt
within his fingers,
works the buttons
through tight holes
One by one,
tenderly.

He wraps the wide black cloth round
and round and round his son's waist
at the birth line.
The groom's heart enters the black coat
his soul the hat
He is readied
To walk within
The fathers guiding light
To the Chupah.

retraces the belt's centrifugal course
walks round and round the groom
To stand beside him
On the ground he laid
Becoming herself a belt
the way story surrounds story
in the Talmud
the way everything blooms
from inside out

40

Deear Michael Goldstein,

I was given your card by a librarian from the Center for Jewish History. I am searching for Mordechai Krengle. He was from Lodz, Poland. He was a survivor, ended up in Israel. This is the last address we have, 14 Ehud, Bnai Brak, Isreal

The eldest daughter
took me by the hand
seated me with her five sisters
opposite rows of fedoras and fur
in a garden of tailored gowns
Around the Chupah
the bride travelled
seven times
an endless veil of night
each step a stitch
Seven times
escorted by maternal Illumination
to stand at the threshold
where the roof retracts,
opens to heaven
above heaven
the sisters draw me close,
whisper in honeysuckle
this be the holiest of times
Right now
generations of ancestors
have descended.
Ten generations
are here in this room
now
and they know
That you
are here
with us too.

reason to believe that if I
reach the family they would not
be receptive
Also describe
how
you are related
to him if you
know

Michael Goldstein BA, M.S.W.
Professional Genealogist
Jerusalem, Israel

I sense fabric, shoes upon
shoes, upon shoes
and wonder if
unseen thread
can really restore
that which has been
severed.

Lynne, I can help you. It normally takes up to four or five hours, to find or throw in the towel. I do not believe he is still alive. I most likely will have to visit the Interior Ministry and see if he is linked to children in the Population Registry. Do you know what his wife's name might have been? About when was he born? Was he religious as B'nai Brak today is very very religious? Also is there a

42

When I began this poem you were old, not as old
as the tree I walked past, yo-yoing for years work to home,
home to work, delighted by its girth and sculpted bark.

If this were a painting, I thought, how masterful
the artist to convey energy both frozen and constant.

Once, I stopped to rest under the tree's generous
canopy and sensed synaptic connections underfoot,
an electrical reach from one street to the next all the way
to the Hudson River and beyond.

That's when I realized that the tree was but half a tree.
     Its eastern edge trimmed and trimmed
        as it grew towards brick and pane.
If there had been no house
     there'd be symmetry —
        instead: absence
        palpable
    as a shadow
I wrote this on a Hudson River postcard with Trade Centers
still standing, sent it to a poet in Seattle.

Ellsworth, your outlines — *silhouettes* — move our eyes
from mere surface to form, plain and simple.
You would have seen this tree, as I had not for years.

I, who pride myself on knowing the names of flora and fauna, and
the secrets imbedded in their sounds, wondered that I had never
asked, *What kind of tree is this?* So I walked to the tree, reached
through the gate, searched for a leaf not decimated by winter to identify.

Elm. Will the tree topple? Fall like Icarus?

Was the postcard with fallen buildings selected with unconscious dread?

43

The old saying — *Elm hateth man and waiteth.*

Would Earth, tilted on its axis, bring the tree to its crisis?

I didn't much notice the Trade Centers until they vanished.

Didn't an elm grow where Orpheus first sang to Eurydice?

He "couldn't live" with her absence, so he courted love in the shadow
world, hoping to reconcile above and below the way a tree straddles two worlds.

The mystery was that it took years to notice the grand elm
was but a half a tree.

> *In this city, distance is difficult to gain.*
> *So close are we   to iron gates and stoops and traffic,*
> *walking on slender   sidewalks set a century ago.*
> *There's nowhere to sit, nothing to stop our busy march forward.*
> *To see entirety, what's required is a kind of break —*

Ellsworth, you gave focus to singular shapes, formed not by imagination,
but by nature's light and gravity — you saw the shadow under a bridge,
an absence, and drew out its presence.

I have walked around your arced sculpture.
You knew, as you made them, that it's impossible
to see what's there without seeing what has been cut away.

We can't stop ourselves from the strobing fusion
of presence and absence that, together,
create a flickering wholeness we've desired all along.

45

Intoxicating — the jack-in-the-pulpit's resurrection,
the Kaddish said daily, three times per, beginning
on the day of dearth, the lantern case that protects
flame from wind. My lateral line? My magnetic

compass? Align me with the poles,

prepare me to cascade into the nearest whatever,
all risks worth taking. Useless as a turtle 'til righted,
I see time running out. Soon the quisling grain
will switch sides, the tallyho of the triumphal
crossing, the hour's destiny held in balance —

Is this over here? Is that over there?

— for but a moment. No Valentine to versatility, the sand

veers in one direction: down. In the end, a vestige

of emptiness remains, spent as Vesuvius, victim

of earth's wandering. The sand siphons

into the next room like a waist in the teeth of a tiger.

The xeric container yields to gravity, yo-yos

to and fro like mercury. Blessed is the hand

that can turn the world upside-down in an hour,

back to our youth with zipless transparency.

O rise and fall —

AS BEATIFIC AND CALM AS THE DAYS OF OUR (FORTUNATE) LIVES...

THE GLASS HOUR

You drink this burning liquor like your life / that you drink like an eau-de-vie

– Guillaume Apollinaire

48

The rattlesnake
severed
by the neighbor

divided
(like lilies)
with a shovel

out of which dashed
a tiny grey
Jonah

a mouse surprised
by light   and air
and second chances.

ENCORE, SNAKE

1.

The furniture is always polished,
the period rooms ordered.

The first room, naptime. Sun
streams in from the alleyway,

I stand in my crib, let down
the slats, take leave

of the afternoon plan.
Pull myself onto a chair,

sneak open a top drawer
I can't see in —

a handkerchief
of ragged white moths

escape, so many I cannot
catch them all

and set the room right.

2.

In the morning, before the museum
guard arrives to turn on the lights,

the furniture in the Shaker Room
shines. No blemishes show,

because there are none, even under
the ungodly exhibition lights.

Nor are there flourishes,
evidence of individuality

which would cause
attention unintended, lead

the mind astray. In the stillness
before the public arrives,

all I want is to
open wide the drawers —

let out the moths.

IN HEAVEN THERE IS NO DUST

52

PAGES 11 & 27 I tried to research the Polish dolls, which I believe were made for the tourist trade from the 1930s on, but found no information. Not sure who made them, how they were "mass produced" with variations in fabric, accessories, hairstyle, and faces, or how they were marketed and sold. They remind me of Rokeach stewed fruit—every jar having a different appearance yet being essentially the same.

PAGE 20 The italicized lines are from Brian Eno's song "Miss Shapiro." The first line is actually "All the peasants in the square," but I recalled it as "All the ladies in the square." When in Kraków's Kazimierz quarter, I serendipitously found myself in front of Helena Rubinstein's house. I happened to be a Helena Rubinstein Fellow of Art History in the Whitney Museum of American Art's Independent Study Program (ISP) in 1978. Let me mention here, too, that I love lipstick.

PAGE 28 Łódź, pronounced "Wootch," is home to the Polish national film school. Roman Polański, Andrzej Wajda, Krzysztof Kieślowski, and other greats were all students there. Łódź has its own Walk of Fame, with over 65 star-shaped plaques in the sidewalk that honor the best of Polish cinema history. David Lynch fell in love with Łódź: "I felt inspired from the first moment I saw it. This city is like a dream." Many films, including some of Lynch's, have been made with Łódź as backdrop. Pawel Pawlikowski's magnificent *Ida* was filmed in Łódź, as was Wajda's *The Promised Land*, about the establishment of the textile industry there.

53 After leaving New York with my grandparents in tow, my family settled in Culver City, California. I walked to school every day past MGM Studios, with enormous billboards of sunny skies. When the MGM gate opened, I might catch a glimpse of NYC or other unanticipated sets. *The Wizard of Oz*, *The Thin Man*, *Gone With the Wind*, and *Rebecca* were all filmed in Culver City. It was also the home of Culver Studios, Hal Roach Studios, RKO Forty Acres, and Desilu Productions. I often recognize Culver City in silent shorts. The cottages where my grandparents lived were built for film technicians, and the city's street names reflect film history (e.g., Ince Street). I grew up to love film, especially world cinema. Remarkably, it is film that connects Łódź and Culver City.

PAGE 29 My grandfather came to the U.S. in 1909. He convinced but one of his sister Taube's sons, Aaron, to join him. Another son, Mordecai, survived the Holocaust by escaping from the Częstochowa work camp just as he was to be sent to Auschwitz. He joined partisans, ended up in Russia at the war's end, was sent to a displaced persons camp in Austria, and emigrated to Israel. I attended his grandson's wedding in Borough Park (**PAGE 38**). The third son, Chaim Symcha Krengiel, died of a heart attack at 33 in the Łódź Ghetto tailor workshop. (Three fates, one family.) He was buried in the ghetto field outside the Jewish Cemetery in Łódź; there was once a wooden marker, but it no longer exists. Only through research did I learn of his existence and find a photo of him on his Litzmannstadt work card. This poem is dedicated to him.

PAGE 43 In 2020, the tree's main limbs broke during a storm, and it was cut down. This poem pays homage to that tree.

ACKNOWLEDGEMENTS

The following appeared, sometimes in different versions, in these journals, with appreciation to their editors:

Natural Bee Husbandry: "Reverence for Bees and Being(s)"

Global City Review: "Unspoken, Ozone Park, Queens, 1959"

Golden Walkman Magazine: "Summer of Snakes"

HCE magazine: "Track Signals"

Naugatuck River Review: "Dear Ellsworth Kelly"

Peninsula Poets: "Early Morning Boat to Ossabaw,"
first-place winner of 2016 Poetry Society of Michigan Contest

Referential Magazine: "Inception" (an earlier version of "In Heaven There Is No Dust")

Tiny Seed Journal: "Black Swallowtail Messenger Poem II"
(an earlier version of "When Are We So Open to Possibility?")

Welcome to the Resistance, Poetry as Protest (Stockton University Press):
"Reverence for Bees and Being(s)"

Thank you to the Atlantic Center for the Arts, where I created the wedding poem collages; to the National Endowment for the Humanities and the Georgia Historical Society for their Savannah and the Coastal Islands Workshop, which inspired the Ossabaw Island poem; and to Summer Literary Seminars (SLS) for the opportunity to travel to Vilnius, Lithuania, to study with Ed Hirsch. There, I met poet Lee Sharkey and friend Anna Kraus, who researched my Polish roots and found our family name, Fajwolowicz. Anna and her brother traveled with me to Łódź, which inspired several poems. Thank you to Jess Stephens and Culture Vultures' Word Up arts residency, which took me to Morocco and figures in several poems, and to Bee Time's Art, Ecology, and Science Arts Residency in East Sussex, England, which led to many bee poems. I was also invited to be an artist-in-residence in southern Spain for Finding the Common Thread, a Bee Time Arts and Ecology Research residency. Thank you to Karmit Evenzur, Jorge Gallardo, Pol Parrhesia, Philip Riley, and Becky Leach. Vasiliki Katsarou deserves thanks for organizing poetry/art collaboration events in Ravenna Taylor's studio (thanks, Ravenna!), which led to "Ear to the Ground."

Thanks to Alastair Strachan, whom I met at Vermont Studio Center, for the pandemic collage that provides the cover image; to Rosette Capotorto, for advice, editing, and inspiration; to Danny Shot for his keen eye, to Molly Frances, for copy editing and hand-holding for 45 years; and to Faride Mereb and Samoel González for their brilliant, designing minds. Thanks, too, to poet and mensch Jason Schneiderman. Finally, thanks to my Uncle Bernie, my mother, my husband, and my son for their love and encouragement.

Made in the USA
Middletown, DE
07 October 2022

12184495R00035